REMEMBERING YOU

THE PEOPLE IN THE PHOTOGRAPHS
ARE NOT THE SUBJECTS OF THE ESSAYS.
THEY ARE MERELY REPRESENTATIONS
OF THE AUTHOR'S WORDS.

REMEMBERING YOU:

ESSAYS OF LOVE AND LOSS
WRITTEN BY MICK BLACKISTONE

PHOTOGRAPHY BY CHARLES AND TRAVIS BETHMANN

For Cindy, 1957-2021

You were the inspiration for this book. Well, not exactly, because, if you remember, you wanted me to write it about dogs that have passed from our lives. I got writer's block until I made it about people. Now, when publisher and friend Sandra Olivetti Martin announced she wants to do a second edition with a dedication to you, I have to find the right words just for you.

I never expected for you to leave so soon. You said you would, but I didn't buy into that conversation. We've been partners, friends, supporters, lovers and just together as one for thirty years. We were attracted to each other from the very beginning…soul mates who often had the same thought. I don't think I ever got mad at you for "doing things that Cindy does"…like selling our house because a friend's son wanted it to be his first house. Or getting another dog, because ours always had to have a friend. Of course, taking in strays or orphans until you could find them a good home. The topper was flying to Minnesota, taking a rescue from an owner who you thought would work, but didn't, and flying back home the same day.

You gave of yourself to everyone who needed you or needed something from you and asked nothing in return. You wanted everyone to enjoy life and be happy. You created situations for that purpose. Especially, for children or young people in our family. A quarter for trying a slice of cucumber. An ice pop on a hot day at the pool. A race on the beach with candy to all the runners.

You made your life seem complicated to others, but it really was quite organized because you could move with a lot of balls in the air. I often watched from the arena and enjoyed it more than you will ever know.

Remembering You is for you, Cindy. And more often than not is about you, too.

With love, Mick

REMEMBERING YOU
by Mick Blackistone

Second Edition
©2022 by Mick Blackistone

ISBN: 979-8-9853477-2-2

Based on first edition ©2008 by Mick Blackistone through Centering Corporation
ISBN: 1-56123-205-X

Library of Congress info on file

Photography by Charles and Travis Bethmann

OTHER BOOKS
BY MICK BLACKISTONE

For Children:

The Day They Left The Bay: Acropolis Press and Blue Crab Press
The Buffalo and the River: Blue Crab Press
Broken Wings Will Fly: Tidewater Publishers

Adults:

Sunup to Sundown: Watermen of the Chesapeake: Acropolis Press and Blue Crab Press
Just Passing Through: Blue Crab Press; second edition, Schiffer Publishing
Dancing with the Tide: Watermen of the Chesapeake: Tidewater Publishers

WORDS OF PRAISE

Remembering You is a wonderful collection of reminiscent vignettes that beautifully captures the meaning of love, friendship, life, and loss. Author Mick Blackistone and photographers Charles and Travis Bethmann have created a work that is sure to nourish hearts and souls of survivors struggling with grief. Blackistone validates that memories of those we have loved feed the soul and enrich our lives. Indeed, **Remembering You** will demonstrate to readers that grief provides a window for reflection and an opportunity for growth.

Erwin E. Abrams
Former President
Hospice Foundation of America

In medicine, we often see a newborn baby arriving on the same day as the loss of a loved one. This is the continuum of life. These pictures and writings in this wonderful work of art reflect a brief moment and a rich story, and help us to pause and cherish the beauty and richness in our lives and relationships.

William Dabbs, MD

CONTENTS

CONTENTS - CONTINUED

PREFACE

This book is about more than life and death. It is about the heart, and the soul…emotions and memories. Perhaps, for all of us, those emotions and memories make us realize that all of those people who touched us made a contribution in some way to who we are, who we became. It is about the heart and soul of each of us…and those who have touched both.

And, perhaps, the words Henry Scott Holland, Canon of St. Paul's Cathedral, 1847-1918, London, England, wrote many years ago says it best:

"Death is nothing at all. I have only slipped away into the next room. I am I, and you are you. Whatever we were to each other, that we still are. Call me by my old familiar name, speak to me in the easy way which you always used. Put no difference in your tone, wear no forced air of solemnity or sorrow. Laugh as we always laughed at the little jokes we enjoyed together. Pray, smile, think of me, pray for me. Let my name be ever the household word that it always was, let it be spoken without effect, without the trace of a shadow on it. Life means all that it ever meant. It is the same as it ever was; there is unbroken continuity. Why should I be out of mind because I am out of sight? I am waiting for you, for an interval, somewhere very near, just around the corner. All is well."

M.S.B.

FOREWORD

Remembering You is guaranteed to bring spontaneous smiles of warm recollections to readers' faces. Mick Blackistone succeeds in jogging our memories to relive some of the best times we had with loved ones, and compels re-examination of difficulties experienced on life's journey.

Mick Blackistone captures the essence of the impact of parents and lovers, spouses and friends, in a manner that is both life-affirming and comforting. Coping with the reality of human mortality is a central theme of this book. It yields clues to successfully struggling with loss, to the strength of spirit in all of us, and to the universality of feelings of loss that occur each time a family member or friend dies. The reminiscences contained in this book span the full range of experiences, touching the innermost thoughts of readers. *Remembering You* explores the importance that recollections play in coming to peace with loss, while ensuring that memories continue to be a positive influence on survivors.

This book of recollections serves as an inspiring example of the importance of acknowledging the good deeds of loved ones that live on as inspiration and motivation.

Erwin E. Abrams
Former President and Chief Executive Officer
Hospice of the Chesapeake

ACKNOWLEDGEMENTS

My deep appreciation goes to Sandra Olivetti Martin, Jennifer Curtis, Lois Nutwell, Janet Sieff and Suzanne Shelden…writers, editors, designers in their own rights who helped greatly and cheered on this endeavor from the beginning; to Erwin Abrams, an untiring champion of Hospice, who encouraged me from the first draft; and to my wife, Cindy, who asked me to write this book and remained my most ardent supporter and critic.

M.S.B.

1

THE PAGES OF YOUR BOOK

Almost half a century has passed since you last sat in your chair subconsciously humming a peaceful lullaby that had no name. You slowly turned the pages of your book…the one I got you from the new bookmobile that came weekly down country roads to fill you with quiet pleasure. That was your chair. Day in and day out you sat in that chair humming and turning the pages of your book.

I can still see you sitting there. You only paused when our flock of boys ran through the front door. You stopped reading to listen patiently to tales of our latest adventures, smiling at our imaginations, until our energy got the best of us and we had to move on…to slay some more dragons.

I don't remember much about when you cleaned the house, cooked the meals, helped with homework, or did any of the mundane exercises that consumed our days. I only vividly remember the most important image in my life: your chair, your lullaby, your book and your unwavering attention, shrouded in a smile, for a flock of boys when we ran through the front door.

2

I was too young and naïve to know what to expect. The small country church, surrounded by tobacco fields and gravestones of our ancestors, was overflowing with relatives and friends I didn't know. I sat with the shaken stability of my father and older sisters.

You and I were too young for this.

I listened to hymns sung by strangers and words spoken by strangers as my own questions and misgivings carried me through the service…that couldn't be about you. I removed myself from reality until strangers brought you past our pew. My world collapsed around me and I collapsed with it. You and I were too young for this.

Back at the farm I heard them say the service was beautiful. They said you were beautiful. I asked, "what do we do now?" Father said, "we act strong, we move on, and we do what your mother would want us to do." I walked away wondering what that meant. How could I do that without you? Why didn't I have more time to get to know you and for you to know me?

Then a hand touched my shoulder. The old farmer, in his Sunday blue polyester suit, stood before me and shook my hand. The powerful hand of a powerful man with pale gray eyes and brown skin worn from wind and sun. He looked at me and said in a quiet, unassuming voice: "I knew your mother all my life. She didn't have much in the way of things, not even a driver's license, but that wasn't important to her. She had her family, and most of all she had you. And she had a room full of dreams for you. You live her dreams and make them true. And you remember this: Your mother was a diamond in the rough, ain't a finer person anywhere on this earth…and she was yours. Now, pick your head up and go get a piece of that good chicken. It's alright now." And it was.

WORDS SPOKEN BY STRANGERS

3

All I ever really wanted, needed, was to hear you say you loved me. I wanted to make peace before it was too late, and I'm glad now that I made the trip. At this stage in my life, and yours, we had to make things right, didn't we? I know it was hard on you to see me, face to face, after so many years and to have me confront you with so many important questions. Why we let it go this long I'll never know and, in retrospect, I guess we were far too stubborn and defiant to confront our individual pain.

It would have been so much easier years ago if you had just said "I love you and I'm sorry" instead of both of us walking around wondering about it. Of course, I know now that I could have said "I love you, too." Maybe that would have helped.

I was hurt and angry for a long time you know…just because you were so stubborn and defiant. You couldn't say, "I love you." All I ever wanted from you was acceptance and your love, nothing more. I didn't need anything else from you. I'm not angry any more.

I've let that go.

Now as I say good-bye to you, I feel at peace, and I hope you do too. It really wasn't so hard, was it? A few words and a lifetime of pain, question, and confusion finally disappears. I've let that go. Now we can both move on in our own way, wrapped in a cloak of final contentment.

Thank you.

MAKE PEACE

4

The news media was filled with commentary today, September 11…the anniversary of the devastating terror attack on our country and our citizens. Firemen, policemen, family members, dignitaries all had something to say as tears fell. So many suffered that fateful day, so many were remembered.

I didn't know them, but I knew you. You left your path that day but few knew about it and, perhaps, only a few will remember that this is your "anniversary" as well. I thought for a minute that I could go on the news and talk about you, but the producers would probably ask what's the significance of your passing? Was it dramatic in some way? Was it connected to the Twin Towers, Pentagon or the airplane that went down? I would have to say "No, he wasn't there. He was in our own town. He was just a man, but he was important to a handful of people…more than you'll ever know."

They didn't know that you volunteered here, or that you carried fish and vegetables to the poor people down the hill; that you cut the grass for the widow across the field; that you never missed your granddaughter's soccer games…that you helped the paper boy fix a flat…that you taught the children how to catch crabs off the pier…that you were never too busy for your family or your church…that you gave your last five dollars to a friend who needed gas…that you carried firewood and left it on the porch unannounced for the crippled man down the dirt road…or that you loved your country as much as the next man. The media executives don't know this. They didn't know you. But I did, and I loved you very much. I'm remembering those who died during the terrorist attacks today…and I'm remembering you.

9-11

5

I hated your work. It took you away from me. You didn't have any real hobbies. You didn't go out to eat. You didn't seem to have much fun. Not that you were unhappy...

To the contrary, you were so much fun for us to be around that I hated when you were gone.

I know how hard you worked for us. I could see that your hands bled, your skin cracked, your eyes were bloodshot from exhaustion, your hair turned gray. And yet you still found time to make us laugh. No man worked harder to keep his children from working as hard as he did, that's what the neighbors said, anyway. You didn't want us to follow in your muddy footsteps. You wanted us to have a way out.

But, you see, when I was young I didn't understand what you were doing.

I thought you liked your work better than you liked me. And I hated your work. I was jealous of it. What was so great about it, anyway? All it did was beat you down.

Then, as I grew older, I realized that it wasn't what you wanted to do, it was what you had to do...for us. You made so many sacrifices to assure us opportunities...looking back, I'm grateful for what you taught me. To work hard and provide for my family and those in need...and still find time to be fun for them. I hope I haven't let you down.

SACRIFICES

BOURBON AND ASPIRIN

6

I knew from your telephone call that you were scared. On the drive to see you I wondered what I would do to help you. You were my father and I was too young to know about this fear. It didn't matter, though. I would be with you.

When I walked in you were sitting on your couch. The *Washington Post* was at your side and your cigarette burned patiently in the ashtray.

"Hey, you all right? What's the matter?" I asked with as much confidence as I could muster.

"Sit down here," you responded. "I don't feel well. Your mother…I feel like I might die…" you said. Your hands shook, your breathing was fast but weak.

"No, you're not. Come on, don't worry. You want me to get you something?"

"No. Just sit here and tell me what you did today. Don't leave me alone."

"I'm not going anywhere. Let's have a cigarette," I said.

I talked about the latest news, my work, and I asked you repeatedly if you felt better…so that I would feel better and not speculate whether to call the doctor or see how this panned out.

You interrupted our conversation saying, "go into the kitchen and take that Tupperware glass, pour two inches of bourbon in it, no water, and bring it to me with a couple of aspirin. I'll take that and take a nap. You can go home."

I did as you requested, and as you drank the bourbon I told you I would stay.

"No. You can go home. I'm going to sleep now. Thanks for coming down. You gave me what I needed."

I left feeling confident that you would be okay. It would be the first of many visits where a glass of bourbon and a couple of aspirin calmed you from your fears…until even that medicine couldn't help any more.

7

A $2.00 BET

You took me to the racetrack once. I was proud to go with you and to see what you saw so often. I was in your environment among the horses, the jockeys, the paddock, the crowds. What a sight to behold!

For that afternoon, I wanted to be like you and pick a winner. I knew I couldn't do it without you and I was hoping that you would tell me how to bet and the horse to bet on. That way I'd have a better chance of winning. But you surprised me, and I was instantly disappointed. I thought we were partners, but I was wrong.

Oh, you explained the program and how to read the horses, the turf, the conditions, the jockeys, all the stuff you need to know to really hope for the best…but you didn't tell me which horse to pick for my $2.00 bet. I only had $10, and I had to have a pretzel and Coke. Winning was essential.

I begged for your advice, your pick, but you kept encouraging me to pick the one I thought had the best chance.

"How can I know for sure?" I asked.

"You can't, but put all your information together and make the best choice, the best decision, and hope the horse lives up to your expectations," you explained.

"Which one are you picking to win?" I asked back.

"Ah, I'm not sure yet. You go ahead, pick one, and place your bet," you responded.

"Come on! Who are you picking?" I pleaded for direction.

"Can't say. You pick yours and then I'll go bet," was your reply.

I picked one and my horse lost. You picked one and your horse won.

I was upset and told you that you could have told me the horse you picked and then I would have won some money.

You reply was a lesson: "If I told you the horse that I was picking, and he won…which he did…you would not have contributed to your victory or won on your decision from the information before you. If I had done it for you, all you would have won is a few dollars which doesn't amount to a hill of beans. In all your decisions, win or lose, process all the information you can, add in your gut feelings, and go with them. Some will be right and some will be wrong…but they will be yours. You didn't win any money on that race but you might on the next. Think about it, and think about how bad you want that soda and pretzel."

8

HANDS

I always look at your hands and wonder where they've been. Your knuckles and liver spots blend in with a deep tan and wrinkles. Calluses seem as thick as shoe leather.

Your hands relive the stories I knew as a boy and fought many wars for you. Your own "wars," I suspect. They said when you were younger you were a big man. They said you never lost a fight and always stood up for the "little guy." I admired you, your courage "under fire," and your hands. Eight decades and they still speak volumes, even though they shake constantly from the Parkinson's. I don't know if anyone else notices.

They said you almost killed a man in a bar. They said you would have beaten up four men at the river for trespassing on the farm. They said you laid a man out on the street for being drunk and disrespectful to a woman he bumped into on the curb. They said you made a man get off the trolley for not giving up his seat to a pregnant woman. They told a lot of stories about you. You told a lot, too. As boys we were fascinated by each one. You were our Lancelot in the shadows.

I never experienced the raw end of the back of your hand. You were too old, and I was too fast. I suppose, too, you were gentler then. Age does that. As you lie here, helpless, struggling to pull the thin cotton sheet over your tired body, your hands still speak volumes. If the nurses and doctors only knew…

9

PIT STOP TO HEAVEN

You had to break your hip, didn't you? It put you here in this impersonal place Jim calls a pit stop to heaven…your emotions tell me you feel this way, too…but you know you can't leave. You're trapped in your own body. Trapped in your own mind. But you seem to have made a transition from fear to acceptance and it seems I have too…even though we don't like it much.

I know you aren't yourself here. Your green eyes no longer sparkle as they get ready to tell another story. Your body is slight and your hip hurts. Your hands don't hold the familiar smoke. Your voice is weak; doesn't command the presence of the room.

Your stories told me who you were. They defined your life and they defined mine. I remember sitting up, listening, as you "held court" from the lawn chair in our front yard as neighbors circled around you listening and laughing uncontrollably. Mother would insist we come in to bed, but you always managed to buy us another hour. Children, those fortunate enough to stake out a piece of ground before their mothers called, anxiously hoped you would buy them time, too. We listened as you spun one tale after another. It was a magical time for children and adults…

You touched us all for three quarters of a century, but I feel this impersonal place, which I hate, may take your last story from you.

OATH OF FRIENDSHIP

10

We ran through the woods like rabbits and hid just as well when we heard someone on the path ahead of us. The woods, our sanctuary from the issues of the world, was our second home. We knew every fallen tree across the creek, every oak worth hiding behind, every trail from here to there, and where we could conceal ourselves for a hundred years if necessary. The Russians would never find us. For over a decade we used the woods to share our first cigarettes, look at dirty magazines, talk about what concerned us, and laugh about what didn't.

When you went away to school you said, "Old friends never really say good-bye." But you didn't know, and I didn't know you wouldn't ever come home again. What am I supposed to do now? Who am I going to talk to when I'm confused, when I want bragging rights, when I need to vent, when I'm alone? You were always there for me. We were blood brothers, remember? We cut our palms, deep in the woods, to seal our oath of friendship.

But you didn't hold up your end of the bargain. You told me, "Old friends never really say good-bye."

MIND'S EYE

11

You were the last of your generation. Cousins all looked to you as a mentor, even a surrogate parent. We needed someone to cling to, someone to tie us to our past, our parents, our grandparents. You were the best one for the job because you knew the stories. You knew the skeletons in all the old closets and could give us answers to our questions and clear up confusion about the past. With you, the traditions and the answers continued for a while longer.

I remember when I traveled to see you because my life was in turmoil. Letters and telephone calls weren't enough. I needed the real you. I needed to sit in the rocking chair on your porch, drink Scotch and smoke cigarettes with only you. Before you let me unload my problems and you enjoyed your Scotch, we talked about how you quit smoking when you were 81…and no one knew you would still sneak one simply because you could.

I was impatient and anxious to get down to business…I was worried that I would never fall in love again after a divorce and too many bad dates…but you wouldn't rush into a discussion too quickly. You wanted me to relax with you, watch the smoke rise, and stare out over the water.

When you asked how I was doing, the door was opened and you let me in to fill you with my issues. We talked, rocked, drank and smoked for hours, only pausing to watch the water and collect our thoughts before carrying on. I left the next day full of your peace, wisdom, and direction: Don't look so hard for the right person or the right answers. When the right ones comes along, you'll know it.

I took your advice and the right person and the right answers eventually came along. And, actually, even after all these years, whenever I have questions I place you in my mind's eye and listen as you connect me to my past, my parents, my grandparents and the right answers. What would I do if I didn't have you with me…still?

EVERYWHERE AROUND ME

How could I have ever thought you would be gone from my life? You are everywhere around me, in everything I see. I can't look up or turn around without your being there. You are in our grandchildren's faces, the garden, the old tree fort in the backyard, the basketball court, the junk in the attic, the pictures on the mantle, the wood pile, the dog bowls, you are everywhere and still part of everything.

I even made a peanut butter and jelly sandwich this afternoon and thought of you! Naturally, it was our "invention," a triple decker.

How could I have ever thought you would be gone from my life? You are everywhere around me, in everything I see. I can't look up or turn around without you being there.

Friends said it would take time, and I would adjust to being alone. What do they know? I'm never alone; you are everywhere around me helping me decide my next move.

Sometimes it's not so easy, but then I look up or turn around and realize that it's good having you here…even when no one knows it but me.

13

We walked many a crooked path together, you and me. Never could get things straight, could we?

Oh, we tried. You know that much is true. We did it all together. They said we were like one working our way through the world. If one of us was there, so was the other…and I wouldn't have had it any other way.

I wouldn't have chosen your final path…the one you took without me. You thought it was right for you. If we had had more time to get things straight would it have been different? Could it have been different? Would you have chosen a different path? I've been asking myself these questions, sitting here, for a long time now.

I guess when all is said and done, the best that can be said is that we walked many a crooked path together, you and me. Never could get things straight, could we.

THE CROOKED PATH

14

You are my best friend. Somehow, over half a century, we survived all our shenanigans. Facing your father's death; learning to drive; our first "real" girlfriends; your motorcycle accident; Vietnam; facing my mother's death and then my father's; your exodus from the projects; marriage; babies; divorce…I remember them all like yesterday, every detail.

When we were ten or so my father said, "At the end you will count your friends on one hand. Make sure you are there for each other."

Now here we are in this sterile room that they think makes us both feel comfortable. If you saw that red velvet couch over there you'd say "ugliest damn thing I ever saw." But here we are. Your hand in my hand. Your hand that caught a million touchdown passes in the big field, a million ground balls, the baton when I handed it to you on the mile relay. Your hand, the one I hold now for the last time, after half a century, is my friend's.

FRIENDSHIP

15

BEYOND THE BEND

what lies beyond

the bend

       in the road

i don't know

what waits for you

round there

       far from here

i don't know

what stands here

is all

       i know

and i will walk

       this far forever

         with you

16

MOVIN' ON

Happy Anniversary!

It's fascinating to think that we spent over half our lives together. I know that sometimes you wondered how you ever did it. All the ups and downs. The children and grandchildren.

I guess sometimes I wonder how you ever did it, too. You were wonderful with your patience and understanding. Now everyone's grown and moved away. Now I'm sitting here under the cherry tree we planted when we moved in, thinking of you. She puts out a lot of shade now, you know.

They've told me I should go out…on a date, no less. Can you imagine? I can't say it hasn't crossed my mind a time or two, but I never could quite bring myself to do it. Oh, I know you'd say "Go ahead and have a good time"…but that doesn't help either. I can't bring myself to, what do they say… move on…with anyone other than you.

You're still quite enough for me even after all these years of doing housework! When I load the dishwasher, do a load of laundry, vacuum or dust you're right there telling me to do it this way or that way.

How could I go out with someone else when you are still with me? When I'm still doing my best to please you! I'll just say that three would be a crowd right now and leave the movin' on to someone who wants to go that way.

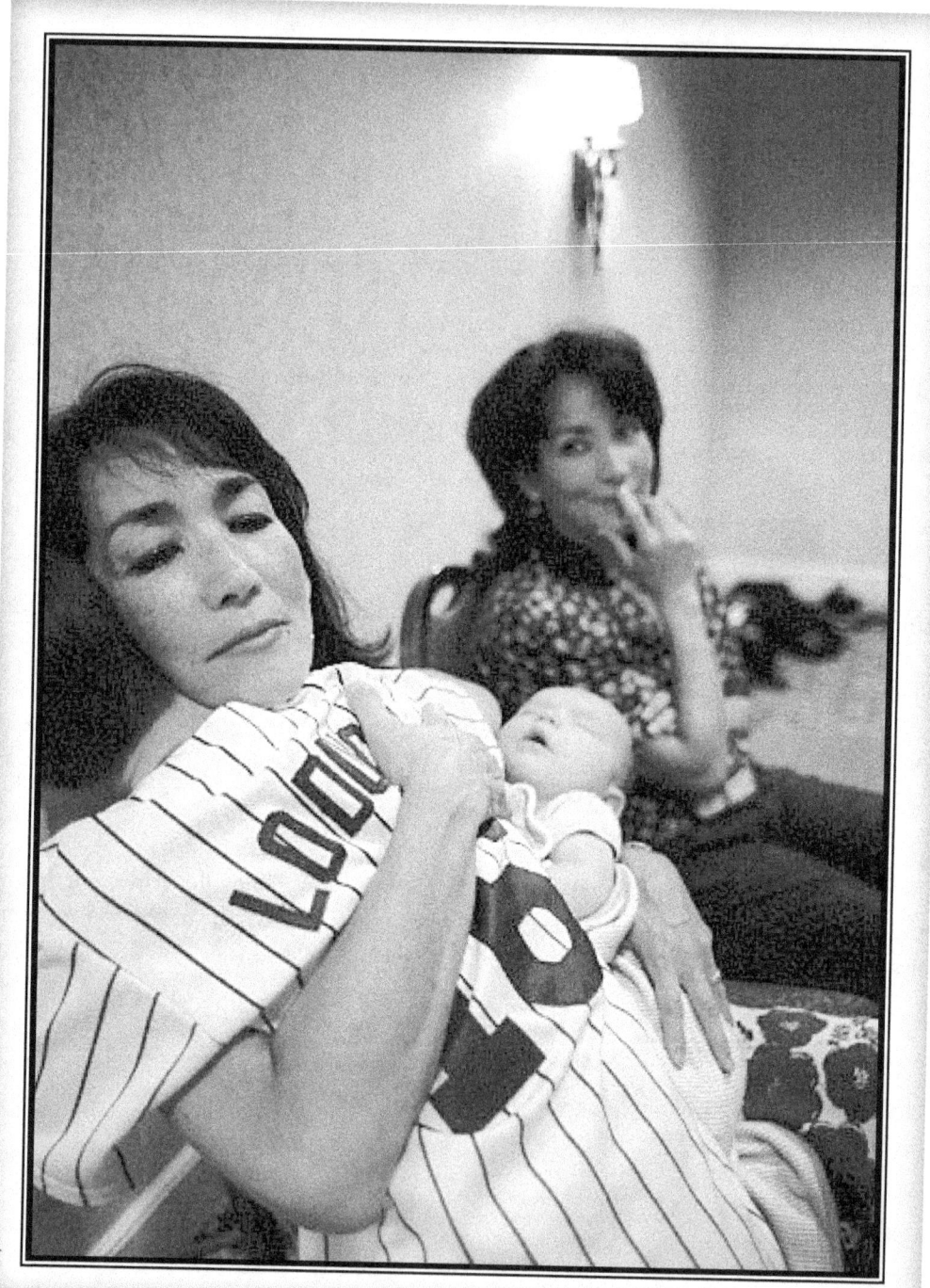

17

You always wanted everyone to be happy. It seemed to me that regardless of the personal cost in physical energy, emotional strength, or money, you wanted everyone to be happy. How many times did you shhhhhh me to let me know that you were going to do this or that, regardless of whether or not I agreed. Whenever anyone had a concern, even over a stray cat, you would step up and say "I'll find a home for it," and that would be your next "mission." We would laugh about it, or on occasion, shake our heads, but this is what you were going to do. Period.

You touched a lot of lives because of your determination to solve people's problems. You couldn't go into a convenience store without someone knowing you. Your reputation preceded you. People never forgot.

When all was said and done, you wanted a party, not a mournful wake. I remembered that years ago you picked out the band. You wanted everyone to have a great time, without you. I never could understand that, until now.

Now I realize that you were about other people. You were confident in who you were, what you had, your own strength. You simply wanted everyone else to feel better, even at the end. Well, we had a great party, your music, your friends. But it wasn't the same without you…

SHHHH

YOUR ROOM

18

Your father said we should change your room around. Make it into a guest room. I had a hard time with that because I guess I'm still keeping it, as it is, for you. Don't ask me why. I just can't let go, I guess. We've changed the rest of the house, but I think your room should stay as it is for a while longer.

When I come in here, I think of you and wonder what you would be doing now. I wonder how you would have changed this room to go along with getting older? From high school to college...you probably would have changed this room a dozen times.

I could never have changed it because you probably wouldn't have liked what I did with it. You always had your own particular style of decorating. It was your "stuff." Remember telling me that all the time? Well, I won't change your stuff yet. When I do, I'll make it into a guest room. You would probably accept that as a "good move."

They say things never remain the same. They say things are always changing. But, as I sit here on your twin bed, nothing changes. When I look at your pictures on the dresser you're still the same. You never change...and I'm getting older...

REUNION

19

We walked into the high school reunion with great anticipation, expectation, and uncertainty. The anxiety was high for no good reason…except for anticipation of how we would stack up against our friends in life's cycle.

Everyone moved to the door at their own pace. Some moved slowly as if waiting ten years for this day they couldn't be rushed at the last minute. Some moved with breakneck speed almost to the point of jumping tables to see old friends. Still others moved deliberately as if demonstrating they were in cool control.

I got a kick out of them because I knew their insides were as upset as mine. I paused, thinking this was better than watching people stroll by on the boardwalk at the beach. Wow, look at him…look at her…ten years and the beat goes on.

I heard Joey ask about "Shack," and he was told he and several of our classmates were lost to Vietnam. Someone else mentioned Emily being the victim of a car crash. And Diane told me you weren't there because you'd had cancer and passed away. I thought, how could that be? We hadn't even had our first reunion yet. We hadn't had a chance to catch up, compare notes, show each other pictures of our kids and brag about our spouses.

Why you? You were the one always laughing, always cheering, always leading, always there for the rest of us. You seemed to have it all…and you did have it all… including this dreaded disease which knows no prejudice and strikes at will at the unsuspecting. Someone said you put up a good fight, but it still beat you at the end.

The reunion was fun, interesting, and over too quickly. You would have had a good time. I thought about you all night and have continued to do so at every reunion for over forty years. You were the first person to fall, but many more have followed since your time. I still ask myself why…

THE GAME OF CAT AND MOUSE

20

Every once in a while I catch myself looking over my shoulder, waiting for you to try to sneak up on me. It could be a noise, or it could be the wind. Whatever it is, it still reminds me that you'd try, usually unsuccessfully, to sneak up and scare the wits out of me. Even when I caught you and you would jump on my back claiming victory, I wrestled you to the ground to prove you wrong. But you never gave up. For years our game of cat and mouse went on, and I never grew tired of anticipating your next move.

The woods are peaceful today. This path is worn from decades of sneakers and hiking boots meandering along. This is where you always thought you could get me. It never worked. I knew you were there behind a tree or rock, somewhere.

The woods are peaceful today, but the breeze sweeping through the trees reminds me that a twig will snap under a high-top Chuck Taylor, and I'll look over my shoulder to catch you trying to sneak up on me...unsuccessfully.

PLAN A AND PLAN B

21

You were so stoic in your approach to things. So businesslike. I said once that if you weren't my sister, I wouldn't be your friend. But deep down I knew you better than that, really I did. I saw your will to be strong, and wanting things to be better for someone less fortunate.

I saw your will to be strong, and still cry at the funeral of an old friend. No one else might have noticed, but I saw you and, at that moment, I wanted to wrap my arms around you and say, "You don't have to be so tough. Let it go. It's okay."

Funny that when we were together and I tried to talk to you, I spoke to the stoic, the business person with Plan A and Plan B. Only the rational approach. No emotion. Plan A or Plan B.

Now as I think about you, that was just a façade to keep people at a distance. It wasn't you. You were the one beneath it all. The one who cried at night, who worried about others, who tried to help in an anonymous way because yours was the show of the stoic. It must have been hard being you. I wish you would have let yourself go to be the person you truly were. It would have been easier on both of us.

THE DIM GLOW

22

I knew you were sick...the flu or something. I hated having to drive you to the hospital for a check-up. Sixteen-year-olds were supposed to be messing around with friends, without any serious obligations hanging over their heads.

Time went by, a short space between the ages, and I never thought much more about that drive or the reason behind it. Just a check-up. It won't take long. Back to playing ball in an hour or so. Life moved on.

Dad said you'd be in the hospital for a few days. Just a check-up. It won't take long.

When I woke sometime after midnight, I had the feeling my brother was awake, too.

"How come you're awake?" I asked.

"I don't know, just woke up," he said.

When I got up to go to the bathroom I noticed the living room light was on. Dad was sitting on the couch, smoking a cigarette, watching the smoke curl slowly up and hide beneath the lampshade.

"What are you doing up?" I asked.

"Is your brother up?" he asked.

I nodded.

"Go get him. I need to talk to you boys."

I left.

Together, my brother and I walked back into the dim glow of the only light in the room.

"Why are you up?" My brother asked.

"Well," he said softly. "Your mother died a few minutes ago..."

We all sat there. No one said a word. I broke the silence. "What do we do now?"

"Your sisters will make arrangements for the funeral. You boys will get through this and go on back to school. She would want us to just do what we always do. Now, go on back to bed, and we'll talk in the morning."

That was it. It was probably all he could do to find the strength to say that much.

We lay back in our beds for an hour or so asking each other questions we had no answers to. We didn't cry. We were too numb for that...Besides the questions kept coming. How? Why?

The next day my older sister told us that Mother had been sick with cancer for many years, off and on. But she had insisted "the boys are not to be told." She didn't want us worrying about her. She thought it was best that way.

I turned my thoughts to the times I complained about driving her to the doctor for a check-up that wouldn't take long. And I thought about the years she hid her pain and hid her fears...to protect us, for a little while, from our own pain and fears.

HEROES

23

The brilliant white tombstones are identical as they run across emerald green. Small flags, real and artificial flowers, dog tags, or stuffed bears make some stand out from the crowd. I think I could find you blindfolded after thousands of visits. It's always good to talk to you. That's why I come. To talk. You may get tired of me, from time to time, but I have so much on my mind and I still miss you terribly. It's better than it used to be, but every time I come, it still seems I have things to talk about.

I still don't understand why you are here. I don't understand why it had to be you. I know it was your choice and you were willing to make the sacrifice, but I still ask selfishly, "What about me?" Don't get me wrong, I supported you. It's just that now all I have is a handful of medals, a lot of memories, and too many things on my mind that were never spoken.

I guess that's why I ramble sometimes. I'm trying to remember all the things I want to say to you and I want to get them right. I miss you and I love you…and I don't blame you. I just wish you were with me in a very different way. Certainly not this way. Don't get me wrong. I'm not feeling sorry for myself or anything of the sort. I still have you to talk too.

They all said you were a hero, you know. I was very proud of you when they told me. I thought about how young you were and what you did. Even today, I have trouble believing it was really you who tried so hard, were so successful, completed the mission, and made the sacrifice.

I was angry until the pain subsided. Then I was sad until I realized you wouldn't want me moping around. So here I am letting you know that I enjoy talking to you, that I miss you, and that I'm still so very proud of you.

MAGIC EYES

24

It was your eyes that saw through a lifetime of pain, worry, hard work and, yes, happiness. The deep eyes that spoke volumes to me before you said a word. I always thought you had the coolest eyes. Everyone else had eyes of blue, brown, maybe green. Not gray-green. When I was young I thought they were magic eyes. When I was older I knew they were eyes of wisdom, of awareness, of life itself. I always envied your eyes and still do. I try to look at the world and see things as you would, as you tried to teach me. But I'm not sure I can be as you were. My eyes are brown…remember?

TRUE FRIENDS

25

I didn't defend my brother in the fight and you were furious at me. I still remember. You weren't mad about the fight, or even interested in why it started. You were only interested to know if we stuck up for each other. You said, "if someone starts something with one of you they will see the two of you finish it." I didn't do that, and I thought for a minute that you were going to "finish" me! I told you that the fight was under control and that I didn't need to jump in to help. You weren't interested in my explanation.

Half a century later, I recall you explaining that at the end of the day, your family, your brother, is all you can depend on to be there until the end.

When I think of you today, your last day, I know what you spoke was true. Your lifetime of friends were not with you for the final chapter when you needed company, help, or a friend. I'm not angry about it. They have passed on or have worries of their own. What I think about is that your family was who you really could count on, and I think about my brother and the fight. I wish I had helped that day…

LOOSE CHANGE

26

I took a nap today and it felt great. I remember taking one almost every day when I was going to college. I took a break for a few years; now I'm back at it. My friends can't believe I enjoy a nap so much and often tell me they "never take naps." I remember now that you were a nap person. In fact, most of your siblings were nap takers, too.

I started thinking about having to rest or nap in the afternoons at the farm. Nine or ten years old and we all, even the adults, had to do this as if it was a religious experience! I remember the times I begged to get out of it and spend a quiet hour or so in the hammock, walking through the corn rows, picking tomatoes, crabbing, whatever I could come up with to get out of it. What ten-year-old takes naps? It rarely worked, and I slept with the rest of you.

By thirteen I was clearly out of the nap mode. One afternoon, while you were counting sheep, I crept into your room, went to the closet and silently but quickly dove into your pants pocket. My goal was fifty cents to go see a movie with my buddies. Suddenly with the thrust of a hand there it was, alone, with the nickels, dimes and pennies, a half dollar. How easy…and how naïve.

At dinner, as we sat eating a summer meal, you announced that someone had "borrowed" fifty cents from your pocket change while you were napping. I admitted the theft. You were not mad but, as usual, you left your message clearly and directly: "If you ever need money, ask for it. If I have it, I will give it willingly. Never take what isn't yours, even if you think you can get away with it."

I sat full of shame and embarrassed at thinking I could get away with taking a lousy fifty-cent piece. Stupid. The big coin stood out from the others. Of course he noticed it was gone. For years I wondered if I would have been successful if I used my head and taken a quarter, two dimes and a nickel. I never tried it again, though. I was more successful with your recommendation and advice. I asked.

Yep, I took a nap today and it felt great. When I got up and slipped on my jeans, I subconsciously put my hand in my pocket to check my change and thought of you. Thanks for all the loose change you gave me over the years.

27

Dancing. Man, did we love to dance…and smile at the same time. We thought we were pretty good, but I'm glad we never saw ourselves on video! You would always say, we're having fun. You were right. We were, regardless of what we looked like.

You loved hitting the floor to the tunes of the '60s, '70s and '80s. And, holy cow, watch out if a real mover came on like "Dance Fever." You were out of your seat, grabbing my arm and pulling me out to the floor. You were right there with ol' John Travolta.

We couldn't sing very well, either, but we did that too. Those were our songs and we knew them word for word. I remember how you loved the folk music of Dylan, Prine and the others. I didn't like it at all, but you made me listen to it even though we couldn't dance to it. You insisted that I listen, especially to Jackson Browne, and you wanted so badly for me to love it as much as you did.

You hated the new music; rap, especially. And when certain songs came up and the young kids filled the floor, you were frustrated that you couldn't dance, feel the rhythm. I tried to get you into the beat, but you would sit and say emphatically, "I can't dance to that."

I'm still dancing with you, you know. The music is you to me. I've even learned to appreciate "Highway 61" and "Running on Empty." Aren't we all?

DANCING MAN

28

It's the little things that remind me of you. More often than not they bring a smile to my face when I find you…within them. A yellow finch, chocolate ice cream, a good wave, a vale of snow, a doe in our yard, or a rockin' song. Actually, the list of everyday reminders could go on forever, I suppose.

The summer rain today reminds me of playing a game of Scrabble, catching the matinee, reading a good book, talking on the porch, cooking dinner, watching the flowers, taking a walk to step in puddles…

They tell me time will make the associations less frequent, but I doubt it. And I enjoy them. Time has made me less lonely and less sad because I have learned to move on in many ways. But it hasn't allowed me to let you go from the little things. For now, I like it that way.

SUMMER RAIN

FORGIVENESS

29

During the last few months you asked me to stay with you a while longer when you saw I was ready to leave. I did, of course, but I think you knew I was anxious and impatient to go. You would lie there and I would sit. We sort of ran out of things to say, and I had done all I could do for you to make you as comfortable as possible. You would lie there, and I would sit.

I realize now you didn't need me to make conversation; you only wanted me with you. You would drift off to sleep, and when I was ready to take leave you would wake up to make sure I was still there.

You only wanted me with you, and now I feel guilty that I was impatient and selfish with my time. I know now that I hurt your feelings and that you didn't want me to stay if I didn't want to...but you didn't want me to leave either.

I realize that I wanted to leave so that I could move about my day or evening feeling better that I had been with you, that you were comfortable, and that, in my mind, you were doing okay. I always felt better when you said I could leave. It erased the guilt, even though I know you didn't mean it. You wanted me to stay just a little while longer.

I know you wouldn't want me to feel guilty or bad, that much is true, but it is still hard for me when I realize how I acted and that you could feel it. You were the bigger person, and you were the one who always set me free.

I'm letting go of the guilt little by little because I'm replacing it with showing others that I have more patience, that I am willing to help and stay without the need to rush away. I'm doing what you wanted me to do all along and I feel better about it. Thank you for teaching me, and forgiving me yet again, how to be a better person at your expense.

478 DAYS

30

Four hundred and seventy-eight days. It's been 478 days since we said good-bye. It seems like yesterday and here we are, you and me. Sometimes, I imagine you are on a trip and will come walking in the door at any moment to surprise me with that sheepish grin that always turned to a smile.

There are nights when the telephone rings, and I imagine it's you. Crazy, isn't it? Well, some people would think I'm crazy but, me, I just think I'm holding on to you. Four hundred and seventy eight days might be too long to hold on, but I suppose that depends on one's perspective.

I'm not sad anymore. I'm not angry anymore. I'm content with where I am, and I really do know where you are…What's wrong with having a fantasy now and again? I don't get disappointed when it's not you coming through the door or on the other end of the telephone. I just hold on for a fleeting moment and imagine you. It's a good feeling, and it makes me smile and laugh at myself. Sometimes I even say something to myself to hold you for a split second before reality kicks in and it's someone else…one of the kids, a neighbor, a friend.

Four hundred and seventy eight days. Tomorrow will be 479, and nothing much will change. I'm fine, and you're fine. We're fine. And, who knows, it might just be you coming through the door with a grin on your face or on the other end of the telephone…well, for a second anyway…and then reality will set in. Then it will be 480…

GONE 2 THE DOGS

31

You could say I've gone to the dogs! Not literally, of course, but I have committed myself to my four-legged friends. You would, I know, think I've lost my mind. What started out as a small companion in this old house has turned into three-ring circus. I keep thinking I'm the ringmaster, but they have proven me wrong too many times...all four of them!

Oh, I know how frustrated you would be with me to have dogs running all over the place. At the same time, I know you wouldn't keep me from them because it makes me happy. You were always so good that way. I never paid any attention to you when you said *No* to one of my ideas because I always knew you didn't really mean it. When I knew you really meant it, I would put that idea on ice for another time. It was a funny, loving game we played, wasn't it?

Anyway, the dogs fill such a void in this house. I talk to them; when I leave and come home they are always so excited, and they make me laugh. Not much was working for me before I got the first one, a loveable Jack Russell I call Scooter. Then I just started adding to the family. I love having them around, and the kids do, too. Sometimes I think I've put them in front of our friends. How strange is that? I can't help it, though, and they are so grateful. All they want to do is please me, and now I hate leaving them.

Years ago when we had that ol' loveable mutt, Jesse, and I got on your nerves so bad because I wouldn't leave him, wanted to walk him all the time, and spent all our extra money on the vet, toys and dog beds, you told me a thousand times in that poor-pitiful-me voice, "When I come back I want to be your dog." Well, guess what? You kind of remind me of Tucker, that big ol' yellow Lab sleeping on the couch, waiting for something to eat. Makes me chuckle just to think about it. In fact, I may just change his name to Jack. I love you...both.

STRENGTH AND INSPIRATION

32

Whenever I hear the song "You Are The Wind Beneath My Wings," I think of you. I sent you so many emails and little love notes telling you that you were my strength and my inspiration. That song gave me the enthusiasm to drive on with every project. Well, the song and knowing you supported me every step of the way.

When I said good-bye to you, I felt the wind fail. I didn't want it to be that way, but it was gone. I didn't flap aimlessly in circles. If I had, I would have made a nosedive. The funny thing was that the projects, the work, kept coming, but I wasn't responding. I prayed that clients would stop calling. Can you believe that? The phone kept ringing, but I could not rise out of the doldrums. There wasn't a puff of air for me to float on.

One day I was so low that I felt paralyzed. Then, I looked up to the clouds and realized that you were with me…to lift me up…and always would be…I began to take off, slowly at first, but steady and before long I was soaring. I responded, you responded, we responded.

I'm still soaring because you are still my strength and inspiration. Like you always said, "We can do anything if we put our minds to it and do it together as a team." Well, we're still a team after all these years and you're still the wind beneath my wings…

FAMILIAR STRANGER

33

through it all
you were there
    when I needed you
    the most
when
    my vision blurred
and
    my voice cracked
you were there
when
    my strength failed
and
    my heart ached
you were there
surrounded
by familiar strangers
i knew
    i could always
count on you…
        and still do
        even now

34

I don't remember you.

I was too young, and as hard as I try to remember I can't seem to do it. I wish I could because there are lots of times I wish you were with me. Everyone talks about you, and I listen to them talk; proud that, through them all, you were my Dad. They say I look like you. They say you would be proud of me. I don't doubt them. I just wish I could have known you for myself and met your expectations...

You live for me through what they tell me about you, and I do my best, hoping that you are proud of me. I won't embarrass you...but remember that lots of times I wing it or shoot from the hip, guessing at what you would expect.

I don't remember you, but you live within me and I'm happy about that.

YOU LIVE WITHIN ME

35

MY OWN PATH

Remember when I sat by your bed and I asked you, "What am I going to do?" I was so uncertain about my life and the direction it would take without you. Remember how upset I was with you when you said, "I don't have an answer for you. It is your life and the direction is up to you"? And how frustrated you became because I said the path wasn't clear. It wasn't laid out for me to follow. You told me that you believed in me and maybe I shouldn't look for where a path might lead but to go where there wasn't a path and make my own. I thought you were crazy.

Look at me now. I've tried to make my own path, the one that you helped me create over a lifetime of advice. I never quit, even when I floundered. I guess I've found a way, my way, and I guess that it's okay because you believed in me. So, how do you think I did?

36

THE SUN OVER THE HORIZON

It's dawn and the sun is just breaking over the horizon. The water is calm and a slight breeze carries the smell of the marsh across the bridge as I look out over the Bay. The water moves beneath me as I look down to see minnows and a juvenile blue crab crowding into pools left by the outgoing tide. A great blue heron is standing sentry on the bulkhead. I can't tell whether he's searching for his next meal or relaxing as best he can. The osprey are overhead in their giant nest perched on top of the telephone pole. Yes, they came back again this year and the chicks are starting to fly over the water. The only sounds are waves breaking on the beach, the osprey calling to each other and the clam boat with her diesel purring like a kitten.

You loved it here. It was one of your favorite resting spots for over half a century, and still not much has changed.

You wanted your ashes scattered over the bridge. I remember watching them float easily away in the current. A very peaceful journey to the open water. You are where you always wanted to be. As I stand here looking over the bridge railing, I'm glad not much has changed and you're still here.

37

HOLDING ON TO YOU

I've tried for several days to clean your closet out. Give the shoes and clothes to someone who can really use them. I can't do it. I know you'd tell me to move the old furniture out and turn the room into the office I always wanted, but it isn't that easy. I just can't seem to make the transition. Or maybe I'm just holding on to you.

I know you're laughing at me for being pathetic and emotional, but give me a break. You're not here; I am. I'm going to start with your shoes and once I cross that bridge I'll move to your clothes. Just let me go at my own pace. When I'm ready I'll go ahead and do it.

You think I don't know what you want me to do? You think I can't hear you laughing at me and saying, "Just move the damn things out"? Well, I will when I'm ready. For now I'm just holding on to you.

38

GLORY DAYS

Well, you would have enjoyed the service, the readings, what people said about you, even the laughter over the tears when something funny was said. You certainly would have enjoyed the service, but you really would have loved the party. Everyone came back to the house and there was plenty of food, drinks and music. Your favorites. I cranked up everything from the big bands to the boogy-woogy. As the songs played people would comment that you could play by ear, how you loved Little Richard, Jerry Lee Lewis, Chuck Berry and the rest of the boys…and how you loved to see everyone have a good time. Well, buddy, we did, and you would have loved the party.

Remember when we went to see Jerry Lee Lewis and I rolled your wheelchair right up by the stage? You said there were benefits to a wheelchair! The kids were so excited that you got to see Jerry Lee, even if they had to sit in the cheap seats. It was about you…and Jerry Lee. You certainly were in your glory that night, and you would have been in your glory today.

I keep telling you it was a great party, you would have loved it, Jerry Lee and the boys blaring across the room. But why am I telling you over and over? I could tell you were here with us, weren't you?

39

THE WOODEN CROSS

I passed the wooden cross standing alone in the grass, placed there on the side of the road by one of your friends. It reminds me of you. I felt a pain in my heart as I slowed to notice a stuffed bear and new artificial flowers leaning against the informal marker. The highway men are careful to cut around it. I think sometimes they weedwack around it to make it neat and tidy, the way you liked things.

When I first saw it I wasn't sure how I felt. I knew you would like it and hope that it would remind your friends to be careful, but I was afraid it would bring back too much pain. Actually, now it makes me smile. I think of you, I remember you, and that's enough sometimes for me. I've gotten used to your physical absence, and you would want it that way. "Come on, put a smile on your face and move on down the road." I know that's what you would say to me. So the wooden cross looks good, the bright flowers look good, and the brown stuffed bear looks good…so good that I almost got out of the truck to give it a hug…

40

THIS OL' PLACE

The wood is stacked neatly in the corner on the porch the way you always liked it. Good seasoned hardwoods that we took from the stand of trees beyond the pasture. I let it sit for over a year so there will be plenty of peaceful fires this winter, the way you always liked it.

I remember when you first showed me how to split wood. I was probably twelve or thirteen when you handed me that axe, as sharp as a razor, and the iron black wedge. "Don't be timid. Keep your eye on where you want the axe to fall and let it rip. We want this done before the first heavy frost and coming snow." There was great satisfaction for both of us when the pile got smaller and the logs were stacked neatly on the porch. I still have the same feelings even after all of these years.

There's a lot around this ol' place that reminds me of you, and I'm trying to keep it up. The hay is in the barn, tomatoes and fruit have been put up in jars and arranged neatly in the dairy, a side of beef and several chickens are in the freezer, and the kids are running around helping out wherever they can. We'll get it all done before the first heavy frost and coming snow, the way you always liked it.

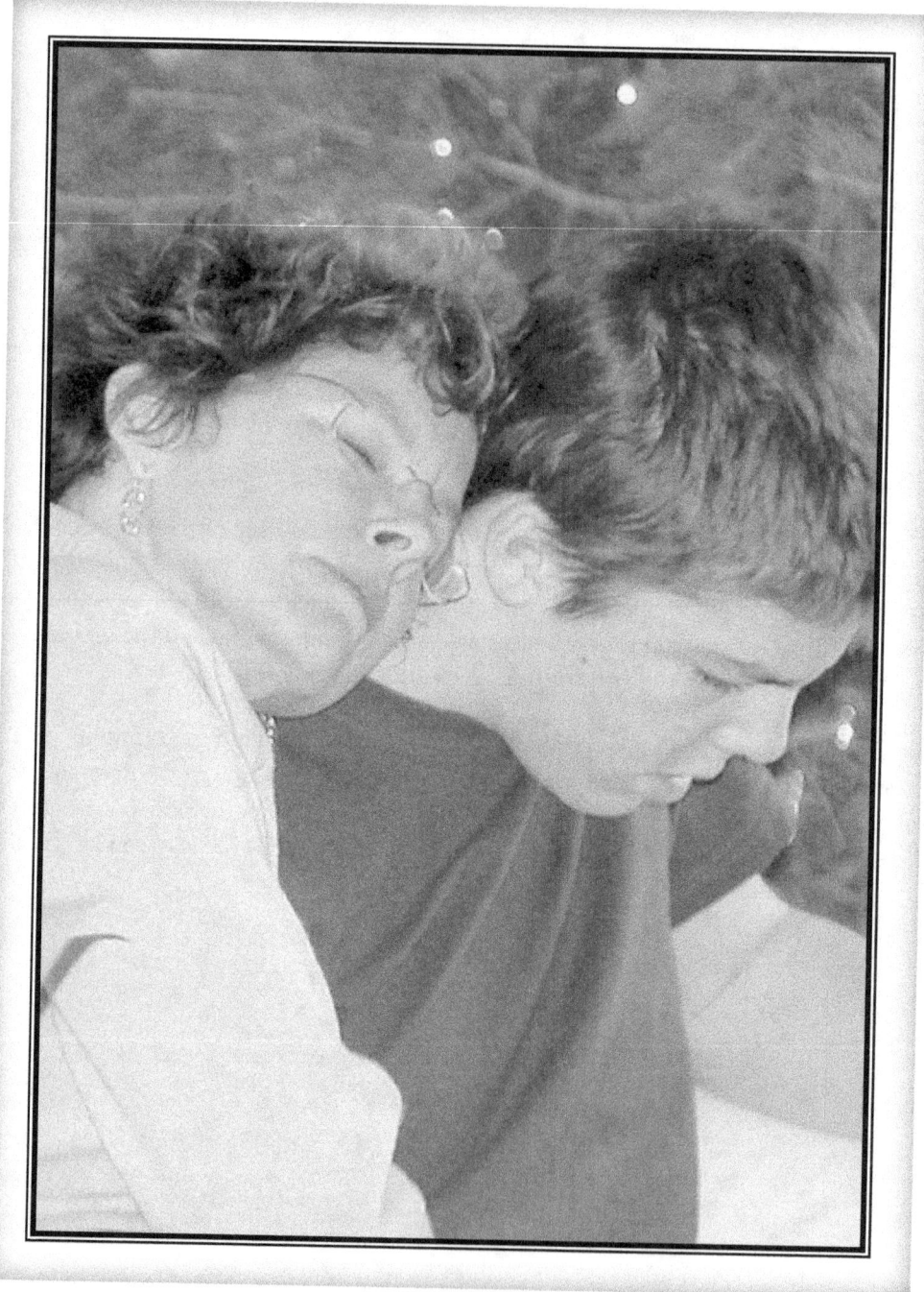

41

When I think about it now, we argued over the dumbest things. Actually it seemed like everything. We argued about everything from clothes to curfews. We had some real knock-down drag-out battles over the most mundane issues. I remember you would say, "I love you more than anything, but I don't like you very much right now." And I would retort by saying the same thing, or worse. I remember once saying "I hate you," and you cried. At the time I was proud of myself because I thought there was some victory in that…I wish I could take it back now.

When I think about it now, I wish I could take it all back and start over with you. Why were we so frustrated and angry with each other? Was it because we were so much alike and neither one of us would give an inch? Was it because you didn't understand me and I didn't understand you? Was it because we never took the time to talk things out? I didn't mean it, but at the time you thought, for an instant, it was true. I know now it was a devastating moment for you. And I'm sorry. I wish I could take it back now. I know I wasn't easy for you. You had so much on your mind and on your plate that you really didn't need me fighting you on every little thing as I tried to establish my own identity, my own turf. I was so immature and naïve to think that I knew better than you. At the time I thought it was worth a good fight. Now, after all these years and especially now, I wish with all my heart that I could take it back and start over with you…but it's too late…

FROM CLOTHES TO CURFEWS

42

The leaves have started to turn today. The cloud cover on the mountain burned off slowly as the sun took its time waking up this morning. I could see shades of yellow and red, brilliant against the green. You loved these first fall mornings and I loved them, too. Leaves changing against the skyline, the beginning of the end of summer, and the woods beginning the end of a new life cycle.

Well, I say I love it until the leaves start to fall in our yard and the raking must begin. I hated it when I was little, and I hate it now. I guess I hate the chore, but whenever we finished there was great satisfaction in seeing the yard again. You always said we could see something good out of our chores if we just looked for it.

Remember when we complained about having to rake and whined about how much we hated the leaves? You would go in the house and come out with some white typing paper, crayons and Elmer's glue and ask us to make you beautiful pictures of mounted leaves. You challenged us to trace leaves on the paper and then color them with the crayons to make our own shades of fall. We got carried away sometimes with blue, purple and turquoise leaves, but you would just smile and tell us how beautiful they were.

As the years went by, we had to keep raking and you kept coming out of the house with white paper, crayons and Elmer's glue. This morning, as I look to the hills and think about having to rake leaves I remember that, thanks to you, something good always comes out of doing chores we hate.

AUTUMN

43

AT ODDS

I felt at odds with myself today. I realized that, for some unknown reason, I don't think of you as often as I used to. I tend to forget little things about you that were in my mind constantly for the first few years after you left us. Somehow, I'm not holding on to being sad and lonely without you. Rather, I'm more at peace and content with wonderful big picture memories of you, if you know what I mean.

Am I supposed to feel at odds over this transition? I don't want you to think that I love or miss you any less, because I don't. It's just that somehow I've subconsciously focused on the positive instead of the negative, for lack of a better way of explaining it.

A while back I think I moved to putting you in my bigger picture without realizing it, and I began to put your values and your expectations into my being. I suppose I felt at odds with myself today because I was letting you go and, ironically, keeping you with me at the same time. I guess I replaced little things about you with bigger things about you, if that makes any sense.

Anyway, I'm not going to feel at odds with myself anymore. It makes me much happier to move on, and it will make you happy to see what I'm doing with my life…and with my new way of thinking about you.

44

BUMPY ROADS

You were hard on me, you know. I guess you thought it would make me a stronger person. When I look back on it now I'm really not sure that it did, but there is nothing we can do about it now.

Your restrictions and limitations made me angry and sad about my own circumstances…especially considering that other kids didn't have the demands placed on them that I did. I never acted angry with you because I couldn't. I suppose I didn't like what you did but I loved you just the same. And I want to make sure that you know that now.

I want you to know that I wasn't that tough on my children, and they have turned out fine. Oh, there were bumpy roads all parents experience. I wanted to spare them the pain and depression I felt in my late teens because you thought that you were doing the right thing regardless of the impact it had on me.

I suppose I still sound angry, but I'm not. I just still don't understand and I still question your love for me. It's the love part I don't feel comfortable about because I really can live with the restrictions and limitations you placed on me way back when.

Why did I wait so long to question you about your love? Why didn't I confront you way back when? Why am I still preoccupied with it when my own children are grown and you've passed on? I continue to work on it and try to understand that your actions weren't a reflection of your love. They really were two different issues, way back when, weren't they?

45

ALMOST FAMOUS

You were our biggest fan. I always knew. I took great pleasure in making you smile with my antics. From your perch on the front porch, you would watch our every move. You watched with great enthusiasm as we threw perfect spirals for game-winning touchdowns in the front yard, cheering us on as if we were playing the Super Bowl before a cast of thousands. You counted with us as we sat at your feet with our catch of fish, knowing that you would get the largest one out of the frying pan. You sat patiently as we struggled through homework, sending encouragement across the porch as we worked impatiently at the other end, overlooking the river while biting our erasers. You smiled when we walked, hand in hand, with our first loves and finally stopped to sit on the steps to share our thoughts with you and accept your replies. You smiled as you held your first grandson and rocked him gently as you pointed to the heron watching us from the shore. You sat stoicly when yet another of your children had fallen to join our ancestors.

Through it all you were there, sitting on the front porch, surrounded by your world. Through it all I was there watching you and waiting for you to speak, smile, wink, cry or gently touch my arm to confirm that through it all, no matter what, you were my biggest fan...and I'm still yours...

46

WHERE WERE YOU?

Where were you tonight when I needed you the most? When it could be only you that could comfort me? When it could be only you who could give me insights and encouragement? When it could be only you who could calm my fears and give me strength? When it could be only you who could stop the pain and give me hope? When it could be only you that could teach me how to reach within to pull myself up by my bootstraps and walk taller than I had before? Where were you tonight when I needed you the most?

I now know where you were. You were within my heart and it was still you who made me feel better after all was said and done...

47

I visited the old neighborhood today. It had been a long time…so many years, decades really, since the last time. You would have been as shocked as I was, I'm sure. The apartments are air conditioned now and the grass courtyards are paved for parking…instead of playing. The big field where we were baseball, football and kickball All Stars, in our day, has been replaced by a Pizza Hut, if you can believe that. We ran the projects with wild abandon, remember?

As I sat in my truck staring at our courtyard, our apartments were pretty much the same: red brick Spartan fortresses, with few aesthetics, sitting in a square overlooking the court. They certainly wouldn't make the pages of House Beautiful magazine.

As I sat, so many memories came back. I didn't see the cars in the court, the Pizza Hut in the field, the strangers milling about on their brick stoops. I saw what we saw: familiar faces, grass everywhere, a football, basketball or baseball lying temporarily abandoned, bushes to hide behind, and our bench. Our bench was an anchor for our souls in the projects.

Yes, the bench with its green wooden slats was gone but, like the rest, I saw it clear as day. I saw us, you and me, sitting there resting, thinking of what to do next, worrying about going off to junior high, then high school and college, wondering what to say to each other after your father died and then my mom a few years later, waiting for the book mobile, Mr. Simon's grocery bus, the ice cream man, or the old guy with his worn-out cart who came around to sharpen knives or scissors. I saw it all. What a time it was. What a time we had.

I left, after fifteen or twenty minutes, and drove through the projects following our old paper route until I hit the highway. I left and took my memories with me. I won't go back. I just wish you had been with me…

SAME OLD LANG SYNE

48

ANOTHER SEASON

I tossed deer apples under the apple tree this morning and now, as dusk is settling in, I'm waiting for them to come to dinner. They are like clockwork, the doe and her fawns. This year there are three with her every evening. Occasionally there are two or three does and even more babies. I still haven't seen the old buck. That son of a gun stays back in the woods and won't raise his head, even for an apple. I sit quietly, as we always did, and watch them until they leave. If one of them spots me sitting there on the porch, I speak quietly to her like you always did.

You would have enjoyed tonight. The fawns finished early and romped in the field. They say things are always changing and nothing remains the same. Well, that might be true for some…

49

THE LONG AND WINDING ROAD

How many times did we run down this road chasing one dream or another? Going from here to there sometimes on a specific mission and other times on a whim to see what we could find? We crawled, walked, rode bikes, drove our first cars and walked down this road again when we first fell in love. Took us everywhere, didn't it? Remember when we would laugh that some nights we didn't even remember coming home? The old road just seemed to get us there.

Now I travel the old road alone…and often think of how it really did take us to our dreams and back. You and me.

50

THE PATRIOT

I'm proud of you. You know that I didn't agree with your decision. Your comment that your personal creed was fight to live and live to fight and that you were taking yourself off the street and going overseas for your country made sense. But I still didn't like it. You've proven yourself now. Your path was a good one and you demonstrated a desire to do good, a far cry from the kid on the corner.

Perhaps, just perhaps, you were less threatened over there than in our own neighborhood. Perhaps, just perhaps, the risks, as strange as it seems, were less in the desert than on our own streets.

It doesn't matter now. You remain a role model for those coming up behind you. You have shown there are alternatives and contributions to be made. To think I questioned your original decision… boy, did you prove me wrong. With each letter you sent home over the months and years, my confidence in you grew. Then, when I needed you the most, you were gone and, again, I was left wondering how I felt about your decision.

Know that I always loved you and that I was with you wherever you were…just as I am now.

51

The Note:

When you read this it will be over so please don't ask questions without answers. Please stop agonizing over my pain that no longer exists. I didn't know I could do it. It just happened. Perhaps it was a way out. The important thing now is that I am free. Free from the pain of confusion, the anchors weighing me down, the tug-of-war between my overwhelming and conflicting thoughts.

Please know that I'm in a better place, even though you are not with me. Now you must find a better place for you and stop asking questions without answers. Know that I am fine and that I want you to remember me and keep me with you...but not with pain, anchors, or a game of tug-of-war within yourself.

It had nothing to do with you. It wasn't your fault. I'm setting you free to find your dreams. I want you to be happy. I want you to move on. Because now you can be at peace, too, and I love you.

FINDING PEACE

52

Our time was full of surprises, good and bad. I always thought that, over the long haul, the good always outweighed the bad. I think you felt that way, too. At least for the most part.

Now, I continue our journey alone and tell myself that the bad is outweighing the good. This isn't so…despite how things seem once in a while.

Hey, nothing's easy. We knew that from the beginning and yet we faced it all, the good and the bad, together. You once said to me if I don't have great expectations, I won't have great disappointments. I agreed with you at the time, but now I'd have to say that life is full of both expectations and disappointments, the good and the bad surprises, and you would say they are what makes life interesting and worth living. You said life is a test, a challenge, and I think you were right. And you said life is a series of choices. The choices we make will reflect upon the outcome. I think you were right about that, too.

Now, today, as I walk down this road, I hope I can welcome new surprises with great expectation and make choices that will capture only the good in every one and every opportunity. It is what we would have done, and you wouldn't expect any less of me now…would you?

THANK YOU

53

it's hard for me

        to know sometimes

where your thoughts are

because

so often

we are in different places

        at different times

i speculate

        then hesitate

and decide to wait

for you to reach for me

because you know

        i'm here

        for you

FOR YOU...

54

It seemed like it was never enough just to say *I love you* after all we'd been through. There I was still depending on you for everything and you not asking anything in return…except that I stay with you for a little while longer. I know now what I must have meant to you, and I would be remiss if I didn't say that you meant so much to me. *I love you* can never express my true feelings; there was always so much more.

Now I'm left with the memories and Monday-morning quarterback observations. How could we think that saying *I love you* was enough? We were best of friends; our deepest confidants; our strongest supporters; our lifelong partners…so much more than love. I shared with you when times were good and depended on you when times were difficult. You were always there. You never complained. You never whined. You gave every ounce of strength you had to help me and never complained once.

I want you to know, deep within your heart, how much I loved you… and still do. You were my friend, confidant, supporter and life partner…so much more than love, but that too.

MORE THAN LOVE

DUCK HUNTING WITH DAD

55

This old duck blind is holding up pretty well after all these years. I remember when you first brought me here and we spent a cold, damp, windy morning drinking hot chocolate and eating ham sandwiches. You taught me the finer points of duck hunting. From decoys and dogs, to insulated boots and overalls, I learned it all from you. Success in hunting, you said, was like success in life. Fine-tune your techniques, be patient, and go for what you want. And, if you don't succeed once in a while, mark it up to experience and enjoy it anyway.

We talked a lot in those days. Not only about duck hunting, but life as it occurred to me. I would go into detail about my various situations and you would discuss the pros, cons and alternatives. Remember that? Some mornings I would leave frustrated at your advice, and other mornings I would leave in tears from laughing at your interpretations.

Then, I guess, we went through a period of transitions, or at least I did. The duck blind played second fiddle to the other interests of a growing man…and I guess you did, too. I guess I thought I knew it all and didn't need you or this old duck blind. I mean, it was fine for you to give your advice to me as an adolescent, but these were different times and I was moving down a road that I didn't think you would understand. And, yes, I thought I knew it all.

Well, I've come back now. I'm sitting here, and it's cold, damp and windy. This old duck blind is holding up pretty well after all these years. I guess I waited too long, though, because we are both lonely without you.

PROMISES

56

I've been taking the kids to church every Sunday, just as I promised you. I know I didn't promise you that I wouldn't sing the hymns, but I haven't anyway. I stand there and hold the hymnal, read along, and I'm sure everyone is just as pleased, especially the children! Remember when you recommended that I not try to sing along, that reading along was fine, and we laughed so hard while driving away from the church because you were trying so hard to be diplomatic about not hurting my feelings. Well, I haven't embarrassed you, the kids or myself! It seems to work out for everyone!

The Reverend mentioned that he was glad to see me in church every Sunday and not just for Christmas, Easter, weddings and funerals. I'm not sure he really meant it because he knows I've been skeptical of organized church. I told him it was important to you and that I promised I would bring the kids. He smiled and said it was good to see me anyway.

I know you wanted me to be more involved but I never wanted to and you didn't push it. You know I get my religion straight from the source when I'm trying to get these crops to grow! It's not any more complicated than The Golden Rule, working hard, and watching your vices. I still take His name in vain when something goes wrong, but I think He and I understand each other and we get along just fine. Sunday mornings aren't going to cure me now. You know that I would do anything for you and He knows it. We'll work out our differences when He decides it's my time to go.

So I'm going to church, taking the kids, and not trying to impress anyone with my singing. All in all it's a good thing. I suppose, if I had to do it all over again, it would have been nice sitting next to you in the pew every Sunday…

57

WAITING FOR THE THAW

The creeks froze up. The boats froze up. Everything's froze up and has been for too long. Why you can ice skate clear to the river. You remember complaining about my leaky ol' skiff every time I had you go help me pull the traps? Well, then you know how froze up it is. I'm as landlocked as that ol' mule that keeps standing there like his feet are froze to the ground. I swear sometimes I think he's a statue.

I hate these days. Ah, I have a good fire and plenty to eat. It's just that I also have too much time to think. Boys don't come around as often in the dead of winter. It's lonely but nobody, including me, moves around. Too cold. And now I swear thinking too much can do you in.

Simple truth is this ol' river shack is lonely without you. I don't have you to talk to, give me hell once in a while, have coffee ready for me when I get up in the morning or come home at night, pick up the messes I leave scattered from here to there, or to keep me warm at night. That ol' mutt can't do any of those things so he's barely worth a damn these days.

Simple truth is I miss you. Took a lot for granted, I did, over all the years. Now I sit, landlocked, thinking too much about how much I miss you.

Ah, it'll thaw soon and I'll get out on the creek, maybe the mule will move, and I'll quit thinking about you so much, and, probably, stop feeling so sorry for myself. The coffee won't be ready when I come in, but the ol' mutt and the messes I leave from here to there will be.

58

I read an article the other day. It was about the five stages of grieving when a loved one dies.
I thought about you and me and what I, we, went through that first six months after you left.

The professionals say the five stages are disbelief, yearning, anger, depression and acceptance.
I didn't necessarily agree with all of them at first but then I began to realize that, for the most part,
I followed the pattern. I sure can agree to the yearning and anger part. Don't know much about the
depression part. I tried hard to understand and to be strong. I'm not sure how successful I was or am,
but sadness seemed to have passed. Acceptance, maybe. I finally accepted the fact that you're not
physically here with me, even if you are in so many of my daily thoughts.

Here's what I know: You were and are my greatest love. I've accepted the fact that you are in everything
that I am and that you are always with me. I'm beyond the five stages. I don't intend to replace you,
to "move on," as they say. Why should I? I'm still in love with you.

ACCEPTANCE

59

I'm Always With You...

I told you that I was ready, that I was okay with the way things turned out...not angry or sad, but okay. We went through all the transitions they talked about after we found out, and I really did come to terms with it. I made my peace and I wanted you to do the same. Don't carry your anger or sadness any longer. It's too heavy a load for anyone, and there is nothing we can do about it now.

I tried my best with you, and everyone. I did the best I could. There are a few regrets, a few things I'm sorry for, and a few things I would have done differently but, all in all, I know you know everything I tried to teach you. Take those lessons down the road with you. You won't be alone. Think of me when you are confused, sad, or even happy and follow what I taught you. Things will be alright. You'll see.

You know, transitions like this are never easy. Change is never easy. No one likes it most of the time. I know you don't either, but it's easier if you have tools to build a new way of traveling down your road. I gave you all the tools I could give you, everything I knew, and now it's up to you.

You know now that life is not a downhill journey. That's why you have hills to climb. Everyone does. What is important now is that you climb your hills. How big they will be is really up to you. Keep them small; it's easier that way. And, remember, when you start to climb one, I'm pushing you from behind.

TRANSITIONS

ABOUT THE AUTHOR
AND PHOTOGRAPHERS

Mick Blackistone comes from a long line of Marylanders; his ancestors settled on the lower Potomac River in 1634. He has kept his close ties to the Chesapeake Bay by involving himself in Bay issues throughout his career as an author of award-winning books for children and adults, as a commercial waterman and as mate on a charter boat. Many government and environmental groups have recognized his work on behalf of education and the Chesapeake Bay. An Admiral of the Chesapeake, he lives in Southern Maryland.

Charles and Travis Bethmann are a father-and-son team taking photographs throughout the Mid-Atlantic region for private and commercial clients. They live on Maryland's Eastern Shore.